Devotions for Graduates

Hester M. Monsma, Compiler

BAKER BOOK HOUSE
Grand Rapids, Michigan 49506

The Revised Standard Version is used for all Scripture Texts.

This material is taken from the *Daily Manna* Series, for many years edited by the late Dr. Martin Monsma and by his son, Dr. Tim Monsma, after his father's death in 1968. The authors of the devotions in this booklet are:

Arthur Besteman 29; R. O. Broekhuizen 14; Jerome De Jong 3, 5; Arthur H. De Kruyter 16; Peter De Ruiter 17; H. Evenhouse 20; E. Furda 12; Leonard Greenway 18; Roger S. Greenway 15; Harvey Hoekstra 2; Nicholas B. Knoppers 8; R. A. Lapsley 13; Tim Monsma 6; Edwin D. Roels 19, 26; G. J. Rozenboom 10; C. M. Schoolland 23; John O. Schuring 25; Wm. K. Stob 7, 30; Paul H. Tanis 4; Gerard Terpstra 22, L. Trap 11; H. Van Andel 24; Edward Van Baak 27; Tenis C. Van Kooten 21; Nelson L. Veltman 1, 28; John C. Verbrugge 9.

a division of Baker Book House Company
P.O. Box 6287, Grand Rapids, MI 49516-6287

ISBN: 0-8010-2939-2

Thirteenth printing, December 1994

Printed in the United States of America

1 What Are You Living For?

Bible Reading: Philippians 1:21–30

For to me to live is Christ Phil. 1:21.

A high school counselor asked a student, "What are your plans for life?" "I want to graduate from high school," said the student. "Then what?" asked the counselor. "I want to graduate from college." "Then what?" "I want to get a job." "Then what?" "I want to get married." "Then what?" "I want to have a family." "Then what?" "I want to see my family grow into maturity." "Then what?" "I want to retire." "Then what?" "Finally I'll die." "Then what?" no answer!

What was missing? The student had no *overmastering purpose* in life. He saw himself passing from one level to another, but never answered the question, "What are you living *for*?"

Everyone needs to have a specific purpose for life. It is one's calling, or "ministry." Paul put it pointedly. "For to me to live is Christ." Christ was the meaning, the purpose, and the goal of his life. He wanted to *live out* the gospel every day in every possible way. And he really showed it too. "Only let your manner of life be worthy of the gospel of Christ" (Philippians 1:27).

Money, success, prestige were all subordinate. Paul wanted to be found doing His will. In Christ he found his strength for each day.

What are you living *for*? To be with the sharpest people? Or to be Christ's joyful servant? Only one life—*what* lasts?

2 *Making the Right Choices*

Bible Reading: Joshua 24:14–18

. . . choose this day whom you will serve. . . . but as for me and my house, we will serve the Lord Josh. 24:15.

To live is to decide. Already today we have made innumerable decisions. Some appear trivial, while others have consequences beyond our imaginings. Today some people will decide what books to read, what TV programs to watch, what date to accept, what school to attend, where to seek work, where to live . . . a thousand decisions await our choice. Every yes involves a no. Some choices will be easy, and some will be extremely complex and often painful.

Among the most important choices will be the friends we choose. A wrong friend can plunge us into heartache and ruin. Temptations to compromise and try it just for once may be suggested today. An apparently innocent yes can ruin a reputation that will require years to restore.

To make the right choices we need wisdom and guidance beyond ourselves. We need to be in touch with God Himself. And it is God Himself who calls and invites us to make that most important choice of all . . . to choose to serve Him. That decision is intensely personal. No one can make it for another. Many choose to ignore or reject God. It has always been that way. Like Joshua of old, say, "As for me and my house, we will serve the Lord." Have you made that definite decision? To drift or delay is to toy with one's eternal destiny. Make Jesus your Lord and part of every decision every day. Yes, "As for me and my house, we will serve the Lord."

3 Good Friends

Bible Reading: Proverbs 1:1–19

My son, if sinners entice you, do not consent Prov. 1:10.

A certain farmer was troubled by a flock of crows that was pulling up his young corn. So he loaded his shotgun, crawled unseen along the fence-row and determined to get a shot at the marauders. Now the farmer also had a very "sociable" parrot who made friends with everyone. Seeing the flock of crows pulling up the corn, the parrot flew over and joined them. The farmer saw the crows, but didn't see the parrot. He took careful aim and BANG! The farmer climbed over the fence to pick up the crows and there was his parrot—badly ruffled and with a broken wing, but alive. Tenderly he carried it home where his children met him. Seeing their pet was injured they tearfully asked, "What happened, Father?" Before he could answer the parrot spoke up, "Bad company! Bad company!"

You know the parrot was right. How easy it is to have the wrong kind of friends. That is true for each of us. The old hymn says, "Shun evil companions...." Be sure that your friends are good friends. The older we are, the more important it is to have good friends. Young people in their teens especially need good friends. It is so easy to say, "Well, everyone else is doing it, so...." But, you see, there are some things to which we will simply have to say, "No." There are places to go, pictures to see, books to read, programs to hear that are not good for us. So when your friends say, "Come on, go with us," and you know it is wrong, have the courage to say, NO!

4 A New Life

Bible Reading: 2 Corinthians 5:14–21

Therefore, if any one is in Christ, he is a new creation, the old has passed away, behold, the new has come 2 Cor. 5:17.

He came into the office of our youth center (The Waystation) with a brown paper bag under his arm. He was a Vietnam veteran. He knew the drug scene intimately. He knew organized crime. He had "lived" a lot even though he was hardly twenty years of age. One of my partners was in the office with him.

Just outside the door of the office was a group of young people and adults numbering well over 150. I was leading them in a time of devotions, testimony, and prayer. None of us knew of the miracle taking place barely ten feet away just inside that office foor.

The miracle? This young man fell on his knees, turned that paper bag upside down, and poured its contents on the office floor. A quick inventory revealed a Smith and Wesson 357 magnum loaded revolver, thirteen bullets, and a knife with the handle wrapped with leather thongs. And this is what he said, *I don't need these anymore . . . I'm coming back to Jesus.*

What was I reading for our devotions? It was the text quoted above. *Therefore, if any one is in Christ, he is a new creation, the old has passed away, BEHOLD, THE NEW HAS COME.*

Do you know about that new life? Your life may not include the dramatics of guns, drugs, knives, bullets. But think of the dramatics of that greatest of all miracles—the miracle of love and grace that has granted to you a *new life.*

5 Forsaking All

Bible Reading: Matthew 19:23–30

And every one who has left houses or brothers or sisters or father or mother or children or lands, for my name's sake, will receive a hundredfold, and inherit eternal life Matt. 19:29.

As a college graduate, what kind of a house would you expect to buy? Eventually it would probably be a very fine house. It would have the latest conveniences such as a dishwasher, garbage disposal, carpeting, TV, stereo, and so on. Yet I have visited in homes of college and Bible school graduates where the floors are dirt, the walls are split bamboo, the roof is thatch and the plumbing is all exterior. Why would a college graduate live in a house like that? The answer, of course, is that this individual is a missionary. This person left relatives and conveniences behind and is now preaching the Word of God to people who probably did not welcome him or her in the first place.

Now why would a person go out and serve Christ in this way? Perhaps for high adventure. Maybe to enjoy strange places. But does anyone really enjoy inconveniences, sickness, separation from friends and relatives? The answer is, these men and women are where they are because they love Jesus Christ and want to bring His Word to people who have never heard it before.

Young people, let me challenge you with the service of Jesus Christ. It is not always easy to serve in a foreign land and among strange people but it is infinitely rewarding! "They shall inherit eternal life!" Here am I, Lord, send me!

6 Right On!

Bible Reading: Proverbs 4:20–27

Let your eyes look directly forward, and your gaze be straight before you. Prov. 4:25.

A baseball pitcher must keep an eye on the catcher's mitt, not on the stands, while pitching the ball. A golfer must keep an eye on the ball while trying to hit it. Likewise Christians must have a goal in life and they must keep their eyes on this goal. If you cannot keep your eye on the goal, you will likely do as badly in life as a sportsman who cannot keep an eye on the game.

What is your goal in life? The goal you have in life will be determined partly by who you are, and the abilities God has given you. You may say that your goal is to seek that kingdom of God, but you should also know how you will seek that kingdom. People are different and each of us must seek the kingdom according to the abilities and opportunities that God has given us.

Having chosen your goal, you must keep your eye on it and not be distracted. Check yourself from time to time to see if you are making progress toward your goal. Examine what you are doing to see if it is helping you to reach your goal. We read that "the eyes of a fool are on the ends of the earth" (Prov. 17:24) and not on the goal. If you met Solomon today would he say to you, "Right on! my friend; I see you know where you are going"?

7 Service

Bible Reading: Romans 12:1–3

I appeal to you therefore, brethren, by the mercies of God, to present your bodies as a living sacrifice, holy and acceptable to God, which is your spiritual worship Rom. 12:1.

Now that you have graduated, what are you going to do with your life? Many young people set out to make a lot of money. Still others are pointing to the professions or graduate school. Such persons may be hoping for a position of prestige and community influence.

How about Christians who graduate? What should be their major objectives? Well, certainly their goals should not be mere success or financial reward, or a position of power and influence in the world. The major objective of Christians should be to serve the Lord who provided so richly for them. Christians ought to express gratitude by way of service.

Paul is appealing to the Christians at Rome to give themselves a living sacrifice in response to the mercies of God which have so abundantly surrounded their lives. He suggests that this idea of giving oneself as a living sacrifice is an act of spiritual worship—the highest and best way of giving thanks to God. But a call to give oneself as a living sacrifice is an all-encompassing call; halfway measures will not do.

The education we have been fortunate enough to enjoy ought now to be seen as a trust from God which must be exercised carefully, judiciously, and unselfishly. John Calvin's motto gives beautiful and poetic expression to the kind of commitment that every Christian graduate ought to exhibit: "My heart I give to you, Lord, promptly and sincerely."

8 Self-Examination

Bible Reading: Psalm 51

For I know my transgressions Ps. 51:3a.

A mother was working in her kitchen when she heard the cat yowl in the living room. "Tom," she called sharply, "stop pulling that cat's tail." "I'm not pulling his tail, Mom," said Tom. "I'm just standing on it. He's doing the pulling."

Thus we put the blame on the cat.

Replace "the world," "the neighbor," or "the church" for "the cat." Replace as you see fit. It is always the other one who is to blame. We are in the habit of "passing the buck" to the other. This habit started in paradise. After the fall in sin Adam said to God, "The woman whom thou gavest to be with me, she gave me fruit of the tree ..."

David seduced a married woman and killed her husband. But it took a full year before David acknowledged that he was to be blamed for these sins. The Spirit of God even had to send a special messenger to bring David to this confession.

We live in the age of the alibi.

But it is time for self-examination.

What did I do?

What did I neglect to do? What wrong did I do?

This self-examination must be done in the light of God's Word with the help of the Holy Spirit. It will lead to the confession: I know my transgressions.

Then I may take refuge in Christ.

He who was not to blame in any respect, took my transgressions on Himself!

9 Develop Your Potential

Bible Reading: Philippians 3:12–16

. . . let us run with perseverance Heb. 12:1d.
I press on toward the goal . . . Phil. 3:14a.

Many young people today are uncertain about their career and their life's work. They go to school, work for a while, go back to school. It can be discouraging to get an education, and then be unable to find a job in a chosen field. Some young people move about aimlessly for years. What is the answer to such frustration?

One thing that is important is that young people ask themselves what specific gift the Holy Spirit has given them, with what potential they have been endowed, then work at the development of that potential with the whole of their power.

What the Bible says about spiritual development, to "run with perseverance" (Heb. 12:1), "to press on toward the goal for the prize of the upward call of God in Christ Jesus" (Phil. 3:14), may be applied to the development of a person's gifts and talents. Not all people have the same potential. God does not ask five-talent performance from a two-talent person. But He does ask development to the full of whatever potential and gift He has given.

Young man, young woman, what is your gift? With what has God endowed you? There is a place for you in God's world. Do not give excuses, saying, "There are no more opportunities," and then allow your potential to erode. Discover what gift God has given you, and put it to work. No shadow-boxing. Get into the arena of life—fulfill your calling with joy. "Give of your best to the Master." Like the athlete, stretch every nerve—for the Lord.

10 Walking Worthily

Bible Reading: 1 Thessalonians 2:1–12

To lead a life worthy of God, who calls you into his own kingdom and glory 1 Thess. 2:12.

Alexander the Great is reported to have had a soldier in his army with the same name as his own. But in contrast to this brave leader, the soldier was a coward. Enraged at his conduct, Alexander said to him, "Either change your name, or learn to honor it!"

No doubt the same should be said to many people who bear the name Christian—"Either change your name, or honor it!" When we are admonished to "lead a life worthy of God," the apostle thereby declares that there should be consistency about our whole life. It must fit the kingdom of God. Our conduct should reflect His glory.

The Lord has revealed Himself as a God of infinite love. Let us not dishonor Him with little love and devotion, but yield ourselves to Him with all our heart. The glory of the Lord shines in His majestic holiness. To this Scripture commands, "Be holy, for I am holy." In the kingdom we are to recognize our King's absolute authority and willingly submit to His rule.

May this day be one in which others with whom we associate see the saving work of the Lord in the life we live. May we walk consistently so that we cause no one to stumble. May we honor the Name we bear.

11 Your Father and Your Mother

Bible Reading: Proverbs 4:1–9

Honor your father and your mother, that your days may be long in the land which the Lord your God gives you Exod. 20:12.

A young man went to college and learned many new things. He acquired knowledge about government, psychology, languages, dramatics, and many other subjects. He met and liked new people and became self-sufficient in various ways.

But one of the most important discoveries he made was not found in a book, nor was it something he heard in a lecture. He discovered, as he tried to grow and develop normally, that he had the finest parents in the world. It was not until he was away from home that he fully appreciated all they had done for him. He was able to see his home objectively—and he liked what he saw.

One of God's important commandments is to "honor your father and your mother. . . ." Each of us should heed this commandment, not only by honoring our parents, but also by repaying them as best we can in loving gratitude. Our parents gave us a start in this world, and we owe it to them to carry on faithfully. Godly parents feel amply repaid when they see their children living Christian lives, studying God's Word, and striving in all things to glorify their Father in heaven.

Christian parents all over the world are praying for their children:

In early days their hearts secure
  From worldly snares, we pray;
O let them to the end endure
  In every righteous way.

12 You Lack One Thing

Bible Reading: Mark 10:17–22

And Jesus looking upon him loved him, and said to him, You lack one thing; go, sell what you have, and give to the poor, and you will have treasure in heaven; and come, follow me Mark 10:21.

The rich young ruler had many good qualities. He had youth, ambition, education. He had position. He had money, the means to bless others. Above all, he had that priceless possession—good character. We read that he had kept the commandments, that he came to the Lord in humility seeking truth, and that Jesus loved him. Almost any father would be proud to have such a son. Many churches would gladly welcome him as a member. Jesus, however, dealt honestly with the young man and, going directly to the root of the matter, showed him that he loved his possessions more than he loved God. "You lack one thing!"

What stands between you and a full surrender to Christ? Face it honestly and frankly. Be thankful if your pastor, or your teacher, or a friend frankly points it out to you. A good surgeon knows that he must use the scalpel, even though it hurts, and a cancer will kill unless it is cut out.

The refusal of the young man was sad indeed. He came running—but went away sorrowful.

Never, my soul, never turn away from Jesus, but, rather, cling to Him at the cost of all else!

13 Vision

Bible Reading: Philippians 3:12–16

Straining forward to what lies ahead Phil. 3:13.

We are to have our eyes fixed on the future—to have the forward look. We are to follow the arrow that points ahead. The figure is that of a race course. The runner in a race must look forward, not backward—his eyes must be fixed not on what lies behind him, but on what lies ahead. This attitude should always characterize the Christian life.

A lad sat in front of an open fire and watched the moving lid of the kettle that hung on the crane; he had a vision of a giant imprisoned in that kettle, a giant that might be harnessed to serve mankind. It was this vision of James Watts that gave us the steam-engine. A man had a vision of men soaring like birds in the heights of heaven's blue. It was the vision of Wilbur Wright that gave us the airplane.

A shoemaker had a vision of a Christian enterprise that would encircle the world, and William Carey became, "the father of modern missions."

It is men with vision who have done worthwhile things in human life and in the Kingdom of God—who, like Paul, reached forth unto those things which were before.

What vision do you have?

14 God Remembers Us

Bible Reading: Psalm 103:13–18

For he knows our frame; he remembers that we are dust Ps. 103:14.

It's scary when you start kindergarten. It can be scary the first time you start senior high. It can be scary when you move to another city and start everything new again. It's scary when you have to go into the hospital or start a new job.

But there is usually someone nearby who tries to understand: a parent, a teacher, a new neighbor, a nurse. Things aren't quite as scary when someone understands reaches out to us.

We read in this psalm that when people trust in the Lord, He becomes a Father for them. And He is an understanding Father. That is why we can sing:

What a privilege to carry
Everything to God in prayer.

Do you know why God understands us so well? Because He made us. There is nothing about us that God can't understand. He took the dust of the ground and shaped us. He breathed into our lifeless bodies the breath of life—His own breath. When He was finished, we had been made in His image. God knows Himself. He knows us.

Maybe your experience with others has been good. God is a billion times more faithful than our parents and our best friend. Maybe your experience with others has been disappointing. God is a billion times more faithful than parents or friends who forsake us (Ps. 27:10).

Remember, God remembers.

15 Choose

Bible Reading: Joshua 24:14–28

Choose this day whom you will serve Josh. 24:15a.

The evening service in Coyoacan, Mexico, was in progress, and young men of the congregation were out in front urging passersby to come in and hear the Gospel. In the front row sat two men, both of whom had been brought in from the street. One of them had been drinking and carried a bottle with him as he entered the church. The youth who led him down the aisle took the bottle from him and kept it at the end of the pew.

The sermon was a simple presentation of the Gospel. Unsaved sinners were urged to see themselves as God sees them, as lost and condemned. God's offer of forgiveness, full and free, through faith in Christ was set forth as man's only hope.

During the course of the sermon I could see that one of the two men on the front row was very disturbed. He knew that he was a sinner and he did not like what he heard. Suddenly he sprang to his feet. He held out his hand to the youth who was guarding his liquor, and said loudly, *Give me the bottle!* He put it under his arm, walked up the center aisle, and left the church.

He had made his choice. He preferred the life of sin. He had heard God's Word and the good news of salvation, but his response was, "Give me the bottle."

There were others that night who by God's grace chose differently. The very man who had sat beside him, who also had come in from the street, was one of the first to respond to the invitation.

The Gospel calls us to make a choice. What about you? Have you faced the Gospel squarely? Has your account been settled? Choose you . . . this day.

16 A Floating Axe Head

Bible Reading: 2 Kings 6:1–7

But as one was felling a log, his axe head fell into the water; and he cried out, Alas, my master! It was borrowed 2 Kings 6:5.

When Elisha was seminary president, the students asked to build a new building. Elisha gave his consent and the young men set to work. One of them, with great enthusiasm, was chopping down a tree when his axe head let go and flew off into the Jordan River. Standing on the river bank, he pointed to the spot where it had disappeared into the water and said to Elisha, "Alas, my Master! It was borrowed."

What probably disturbed the young man was two things. First of all, the owner would not treat him too kindly. But secondly, he was now without a tool with which to participate in the building of the new school building. Elisha, however, came to the rescue. He threw a stick into the water and, miraculously, the iron axe head floated on the surface.

How often it seems to us that God could scarcely consider our little lives amid all the great events of modern times. Why should He care if we are busy, handicapped, ill, or sorrowing? We are just common insignificant folks in a day of space exploration and international intrigue.

But when I read about this floating axe head, I am reassured that God is greater than I usually suppose. He not only sees and controls the great things of life, he is also interested in the little things as well. He tends to the details. He cares for the very tools with which I work.

17 Sowing and Reaping

Bible Reading: Galatians 6:1–10

Do not be deceived: God is not mocked, for whatever a man sows, that he will also reap Gal. 6:7.

In my garden a wonderful thing happened last spring. It was not unusual and I anticipated it, but it was wonderful. I planted a row of tomato plants and a half row of head lettuce plants, a row of cabbage plants; I sowed a row of carrot seeds, a row of peas, two rows of beans, and a row of red beets. Just where I had sown the carrots there my garden produced carrots and so it was with the rest of my garden. What I had planted and sown, that it produced, and that I reaped. This made for purpose, order, and meaning in my gardening.

But here Paul is speaking not of plant life but of the soul and spirit life. He goes on to say, "For he that soweth to his own flesh will from the flesh reap corruption; but he who sows to the Spirit will from the Spirit reap eternal life."

Paul is warning what crop we may expect if we are sowing the seeds of sin. Disobedience, dishonesty, intemperance, impurity, vanity: each will bring forth fruit after its kind. Paul is promising that sowing to the Spirit will bring forth fruit after its kind: peace, joy, hope, life everlasting. This puts purpose and meaning into life.

If you have sown in sin, there is forgiveness and cleansing with God through repentance and faith. Be not deceived by self, sin, or Satan; rather be received by God. If by God's grace you are sowing to the Spirit, be not weary in well doing for in due season we shall reap, if we faint not, for God is not mocked.

18 We Will Not Serve Your Gods

Bible Reading: Daniel 3:13–30

. . . Be it known to you, O king, that we will not serve your gods . . . Dan. 3:18.

Daniel's three friends refused to worship Nebuchadnezzar's golden image. They stood by their convictions, confident that God was able to deliver them. They refused to follow the crowd. They dared to be different so that the one true God might be honored through their faith.

Someone has written, "There is no tyranny on earth so brutal and inhuman as the law of the social mob." Perhaps this is an exaggeration, but no one will deny that it takes lots of courage to be different in a situation where the highest law is the law of the average.

Young people ought to rethink the practice of imitating the crowd. The old excuse that we must do this or that because "everyone's doing it" is threadbare and unjustified. What if Shadrach, Meshach, and Abednego had followed that policy?

Remember this, young people, the crowd is not always right. History proves that the crowd often is wrong. Many young people have started on "liquor lane" because they thought everyone was doing it and they wanted to be "good sports." But that kind of "sport" never is good.

The crowd can get you into trouble, and when it does, it deserts you. Your real friend is the person who refuses to sin with you.

19 Using Your Talents

Bible Reading: Exodus 31:1–6

I have given to all able men ability, that they may make all that I have commanded you Exod. 31:6.

Most honest work is legitimate work for the Christian. Christians, no matter what their calling, are able to promote the kingdom of God in their work by doing it in a God-pleasing way. The work of Christians becomes kingdom work, no matter what they do.

However, that does not mean that Christians are permitted to choose just any old job for their life's work. God has given each of us certain talents and abilities, and He has given them to us for a purpose. We can't simply ignore those talents or just pretend that we do not have them. God wants and expects us to use what He gave us in the best possible way. We may not squander or waste our time or possessions, but neither may we waste our talents. If we have a gift we should seek to use it, and we should use it in a way that we believe most pleases God.

Any work we choose, therefore, should permit us to develop our creative abilities, to use our precious time and energy productively and meaningfully. We should not become prisoners of our work. Nor should we work *simply* "to make ends meet." Nor yet should we slave away at something during the day to make it possible for us to "enjoy ourselves" at night or on weekends. God wants us to be meaningfully involved IN our work and not simply AFTER work.

20 A Father's Instructions

Bible Reading: Proverbs 13:1–12

A wise son hears his father's instruction Prov. 13:1.

A father is wiser than his son because he has matured in judgment and the school of experience has been an excellent instructor. In the Book of Proverbs, Solomon is rich in his counsel, like a wise father who has seen much folly and its subsequent sadness. Speaking from experience, Solomon tells youth to give ear to the counsel of their parents, and the one who heeds this advice he counts to be wise.

William Jennings Bryan was summoned by his father just prior to the young man's departure for college. He thought his father was going to give him a final sermon as a send-off. He was surprised, however, when he received not a sermon, but a simple request. The father asked the young lad if he would promise to read the Book of Proverbs through once a month for a year. The lad made the promise and kept it. Later in life, Bryan looked upon his father's request as perhaps one of the most important factors in his early life. His frequent reading of Proverbs at that period gave him wisdom for practical life. It set him on guard against pitfalls that were ever threatening. It put him on the alert against the devil's agents which were abroad in his day as well as in ours. He later realized that by the reading of the Book of Proverbs the Word was sown and hid in his heart to keep him from great transgressions.

Many of you may be leaving home. Have you read the Book of Proverbs? From the experience of the Christian statesman Bryan comes this advice to all our youth: read the Book of Proverbs, and discover for yourself its stimulus to godly living.

21 Whose Side Are You On?

Bible Reading: Matthew 12:22–30

He who is not with me is against me, and he who does not gather with me scatters Matt. 12:30.

Go to a football game and you know soon which side everyone is on. Usually the supporters of each team have their own seating section. When one team makes a score, those on that side stand up and cheer and wave flags. When the opposite team scores, the others are heard from. Everyone is for one team or the other, and everyone demonstrates clearly which team that is. It is hard to find a fence sitter at a football game. Everyone is on one side or the other.

Jesus is looking for the same behavior in people in their relationship to Him. Jesus warns that no one can be neutral in the game of life. Everyone is either for the Lord or against Him. He is either gathering to the Lord or he is scattering from Him. He is either building up or tearing down.

On another occasion Jesus talked about two ways through life—a broad way and a narrow one. Jesus warned that the first way leads to destruction and the second way leads to life. One cannot travel on both roads at the same time.

Jesus emphasized that there are two ways, two goals, two motives. Everyone is moving in one or the other. There are good and evil, truth and error, God and Satan, the kingdom of God and the kingdom of the world. These are opposites. They never meet nor mingle.

Everyone is for one or the other. One cannot be for both.

Which side are you on?

22 The Responsibility of Having

Bible Reading: Luke 12:42–48

Every one to whom much is given, of him will much be required; and of him to whom men commit much they will demand the more Luke 12:48.

If we want to have the right attitude toward giving, we must first have the right attitude toward getting. That is, do we feel that our strength and skills and opportunities are of our own making, or are they gifts from the Lord? The more we feel that we are responsible for our own success, the less we will feel responsible for sharing with the poor.

Do you know that in many countries of the world there are people who wish they had the resources and the opportunities that we have? They try and they fail, sometimes because of lack of skill and good management, sometimes because of poor health, government restrictions, or natural disasters. We can help by sponsoring or sharing in training programs and, especially in times of disaster, by outright giving.

As a young person, I ask you to think about going to people in some other country, sharing your strength and knowledge and, most important of all, your love.

Your strength of mind and body belong to God. Share them. The skills and talents you have are from Him. Use them to enrich the lives of others. And be careful not to lay up treasures on earth—to build your own kingdom—but as citizens of the kingdom of heaven, show others the riches of the Father's love by sharing your money, your talents, and the greatest gift of all—your love.

If you have much, do not say, "I was responsible for getting this," but say, "I am responsible for using this to bless other lives."

23 The Kingdom — Then All

Bible Reading: Matthew 6:25–34

But seek first his kingdom and his righteousness, and all these things shall be yours as well Matt. 6:33.

I was about 15 years old. I had delivered my evening newspapers and was sitting near my mother who was at the sewing machine. I had a big problem. "What must I be in life, Mother?" How should "make a living?"

Mother turned to me and quoted: "Seek first his kingdom, son." But that wasn't the answer I wanted. That really didn't help me any. That was religion. It meant giving my heart to Jesus, making confession of faith, etc. But that had little if anything to do with my problem. I needed something for this life, something practical, something tangible, not a vague something for a distant hereafter. So I said, "But, Mother . . ." and explained what I meant, something "down to earth."

I still see her smile as she turned again and merely quoted the rest of the same passage: "And all these things shall be yours as well."

How right she was, and how wise! There just wasn't a better answer to my problem—nor really any other answer. I was a child of the covenant, taken into the "family" of God by God Himself and sealed as such, with all the wondrous promises of God in my favor, promised me in the way of faith in Him. There was really only one sensible thing for me to do: acknowledge, claim, and appropriate my place in the "family," anchor myself forever in the Savior by faith in Him, and thus secure my life for time and eternity so fully that "All things work together for good" under the searching eye and guiding hand of a loving Father in heaven! What more could one even wish for!

24 It Became a Rod in His Hand

Bible Reading: Exodus 4:1–9

But the Lord said to Moses, Put out your hand, and take it by the tail—so he put our his hand and caught it, and it became a rod in his hand Exod. 4:4.

The Lord commanded Moses to take the serpent by its tail. This was very dangerous. You've probably learned that the only safe place to hold a serpent is behind its head. In that position the serpent can do no harm. But take a snake by its tail, and immediately the animal will twist its long body and bite.

God was illustrating to Moses how dangerous the coming task would be. Going to Pharoah in order to bring the people of Israel out of Egypt would be like taking a serpent by the tail. Egypt would react in a very hostile way. From a human point of view, Moses took a great risk.

However, when Moses faithfully obeyed and took the serpent by its tail, it became a rod in his hand. This, too, was an illustration. God said in effect: If you accept My mandate, taking your risks while trusting in Me, then you will become strong.

Here is a truth we may never forget. In this world obedience to the Word of God often involves a great deal of risk. To stand up for Jesus and His cause can result in pain and loss. Yet, if we do it willingly and in true confidence in the Lord, we will become strong. Compromisers are always weak, but those who are faithful will experience that conquered serpents become rods in one's hand.

25 For Me to Live Is Christ

Bible Reading: Philippians 1:11–30

For to me to live is Christ, and to die is gain Phil. 1:21.

"Today's quiz," says the teacher to her class, "will be a matter of filling in the blanks. You are acquainted with all of the statements, and all you have to do is fill in the right answer."

Let us take this spiritual quiz by filling in the blanks. Leave out the words "Christ" and "gain" in our text. It would then read, "For to me to live is ____________, and to die is ____________." Now fill in the blanks.

Suppose we fill in the blanks with the philosophy of the materialist. "For to me to live is *to make money,* and to die ____________? To die is to leave it all behind." How would the status seeker fill in the blanks? "For to me to live is *to make a name for myself,* and to die is ____________? To die is to have my name in the history book or inscribed on a monument." The power-hungry person would say, "For to me to live is *to wield power, world-wide power if possible,* and to die is ____________? To die is to have that power return to the dust."

There is only one answer that can assure lasting happiness and eternal life. That answer is *Christ.* "For to me to live is Christ, and to die is *gain.*"

How do you fill in the blanks?

26 With the Help of God

Bible Reading: Proverbs 3:1–10

In all your ways acknowledge him, and he will make straight your paths Prov. 3:6.

For some young people it is very easy to choose a vocation. They have always had their heart set on being a teacher or a preacher or a worker in their Dad's business or a mechanic or a musician. For many others, however, the decision is very hard. They just don't know what to do. They honestly have no idea how they should be spending their life. What should they do?

The Bible gives no definite answers to the question concerning vocations, since times and circumstances continue to change. However, there are some general guidelines which every Christian may follow, and these are worth considering by those who sincerely want to serve God in their working lives. First of all, Christians should make a serious effort to discover strengths and weaknesses. Secondly, they should thoughtfully study the job market to see which fields are open and which are already crowded. Thirdly, they should spend much time in earnest prayer seeking the help of God in learning God's purpose for their lives. Since God wants us to serve Him to the very best of our ability, He will surely help us to use wisely the talents and abilities He gave us.

It may take some time before all the pieces of our vocational puzzle fit together. We may be assured, however, that God will direct the paths of those who fully commit their lives—including their work lives—to the Lord in prayer.

27 God Almighty Bless You

Bible Reading: Genesis 28:1–5

God Almighty bless you Gen. 28:3.

Millions of young men and women are graduating from high schools and colleges in the United States. Millions more join them in Europe, Asia, and Canada. Beyond the graduates lie the decisions and challenges of further education, employment, military service, marriage. And almost every decision will involve, directly or indirectly, the decision to leave the parental home, protection, and security.

This is all normal. There are many ways one can leave home. Tragedy looms large when the departing footfall is covered by the sound of a slammed door. Danger is ahead for those who must stealthily sneak out under cover of darkness and silence, as Jacob did. Blessed is the youth for whom the last sound in the parental home is the "Amen" of a prayer of farewell, a supplication for divine protection.

The day of graduation is a certain sign that a day of separation from home cannot be far away. Some will measure the interval between graduation and home-leaving in days; for a few it will be years. But at best it is an interval. It is certain, normal, and good, that a youth should leave father and mother. It is no tragedy at all, but a blessing, if the preparation has been made in prayer, and if the departure is done in the hope of thus better serving one's God.

28 Begin Early

Bible Reading: Ecclesiastes 11:9—12:1

Remember also your Creator in the days of your youth, before the evil days come, and the years draw nigh, when you will say, I have no pleasure in them Eccles. 12:1.

A girl ran to catch a bus. Just as she reached the station, the bus moved on and left her standing there. She gasped for breath as she watched the bus disappear in the distance. A man said to her, "You didn't run fast enough." "Yes, I did," she replied. "I ran with all my might, but I didn't make it because I didn't start soon enough."

Young people can do great things for Christ in this world. But they need to get ready now! They won't get very far by saying, "There's plenty of time."

Do you often find yourself putting off what should be done today? Do you leave the completion of an assignment until the last moment? You have a whole week to work on it but at the last moment you finally get at it. Starting well on time always pays off.

The time of youth is a time of laying foundations. As in the building of a house, there is nothing outstanding about pouring some concrete for the foundation. It is much more exciting to turn the key in the front door for the first time after it is finished.

"Remember also your Creator in the days of your youth." Before the strong winds of temptation blow, make sure that your *foundation* is a living faith in Christ as your Savior and Lord. Then you are ready! Then you will always have pleasure in the Creator even though the times are evil. Begin now! Start right—build a good foundation.

29 Elijah Calls for Decision

Bible Reading: 1 Kings 18:20–25

And Elijah came near to all the people, and said, How long will you go limping with two different opinions? If the Lord is God, follow him; but if Baal, then follow him. And the people did not answer him a word 1 Kings 18:21.

There is an old story about a donkey that was standing between two haystacks. He could not decide from which haystack he wanted to eat so finally he starved to death. This is a picture of many people today who because of indecision face eternal death. In the scene before us we have a call to decision.

As Elijah meets with the 450 prophets of Baal on Mount Carmel, he sees a multitude of undecided people. These people had a rich spiritual heritage including the law of God, a knowledge of God's great deeds on their behalf and the promise of the Messiah, but they remain uncommitted.

Some people were undecided because Baal worship was so easy. They could worship Baal and still indulge in their pet sins. Many Israelites were kept from making a decision because of fear. What would others say if they served the Lord? Still others were marked by procrastination, thinking that next year or the following would be a better time to decide.

Young people, what about you? Have you made your decision? Or are you afraid of what friends at school or associates at work might think if it became known that you are a follower of Jesus Christ? Have you been delaying, thinking that tomorrow might be a better time? How long are you going to wait? Remember, today is the day of salvation!

30 Graduation

Bible Reading: Philippians 3:1–5

I press on toward the goal for the prize of the upward call of God in Christ Jesus Phil. 3:14.

Four years of schooling are now over. The invitations have been sent to all the relatives. It's a proud moment for friends and family alike. The goal which has been set has now been reached. Where do you go from here?

Well, the first inclination is to sit back and rest a while; and perhaps one is even tempted to congratulate oneself a bit for having completed this milestone in life. There is the temptation to believe that the prize has been won, the goal has been reached, and all is finished.

Interestingly the service which commemorates the completion of those four years of schooling is generally called commencement, which implies not finishing but beginning. That's a good thought to ponder for a moment. What does one now do with all of this education, expertise, and training? The Christian graduate should certainly use these good things as an opportunity, not to end, but to begin, to realize that now is the time to really begin life in earnest.

Paul realized that the Christian has the temptation, once redeemed, to sit back and take it easy as though everything has been accomplished. Paul shattered that idea by making it clear that he does not consider himself to have "arrived" at all. What better commitment could a Christian graduate make than to realize that one's life must be constant stewardship, always pressing forward and onward and upward to do the work of Christ our mentor, our Savior, our King.